DELIVERING SUCCESSFUL PROJECTS

The Universal Manager

ACKNOWLEDGEMENTS

This publication was developed by Scitech Educational in partnership with NEBS Management.

Project management:	Diana Thomas (NEBS Management)
	Don McLeod (Scitech Educational)
Series editor:	Darren O'Conor
Authors:	William Aitken, Darren O'Conor

Dossier 02: Delivering Successful Projects

A Scitech Educational publication

Distributed by Scitech-DIOL

ISBN 0 948672 77 3

Published by:
Scitech Educational Ltd
15 – 17 The St John Business Centre
St Peter's Road
Margate
Kent CT9 1TE
Tel: +44 (0)1843 231494
Fax: +44 (0)1843 231485
Website: www.universal-manager.co.uk
            http://www.scitechdiol.co.uk

CONTENTS

DELIVERING SUCCESSFUL PROJECTS

THE UNIVERSAL MANAGER SERIES

Books

01 **Risk Management**
02 **Delivering Successful Projects**
03 **Planning and Controlling Projects**
04 **The Learning Organization**
05 **Managing for Knowledge**
06 **Obtaining and Retaining Customers**
07 **Human Resource Planning**
08 **Business Planning**
09 **Financial Performance**
10 **Managing Quality**
11 **Business Relationships**
12 **Managing for High Performance**
13 **Managing Harmoniously**
14 **21st Century Communication**
15 **Managing for Sustainability**

Computer-based Resources

Management Assignments (CD-ROM)
Personal Developing Planning Toolkit
        (at www.universal-manager.co.uk)
Learning Styles Toolkit
        (at www.universal-manager.co.uk)

PREFACE

Today, the concept of project management enjoys greater visibility and credibility than ever before. The tools and techniques of the discipline have spread far beyond the industry sectors that developed them, and are now just as likely to be employed within a bank or hospital as in a construction or manufacturing company. Project management textbooks and software packages are available in abundance, and there is no shortage of training and consultancy for organizations and individuals who want to learn how it should be done.

There is however a downside to this increasing awareness and buy-in to project management principles. Every sector, every textbook and every software programme seems to have its own unique take on project management — divergence can be found even on fundamental matters such as the definition of key terms (project, programme, design, build, etc.). Round up half a dozen project managers from different backgrounds, leave them to talk for a few minutes, and before long you will have utter confusion. It is not simply that terminologies vary. Even more problematic is that project managers tend to 'specialize' in what they consider to be the essential aspect of project management — for most this is planning, but many focus on the front end definition of a project before detailed planning begins, while others may concentrate on the political realm (relationship building, maintaining a high profile, and so on).

The Universal Manager series attempts to take a balanced view of the total discipline in two dossiers:

- ☞   02   Delivering Successful Projects
- ☞   03   Planning and Controlling Projects.

This dossier, *Delivering Successful Projects*, concentrates on what might be considered the 'softer' project management skills: initiating and scoping projects, establishing feasibility, building the project team and dealing with the key players.

It also explores the evolution of project management theory from post-war US Department of Defence developments, to the more recent concepts of 'lean thinking' and 'modified design'.

Its companion, *Planning and Controlling Projects*, examines the 'harder' skills which come into play after project start-up: contracting; planning and scheduling; monitoring, review and evaluation. Key techniques discussed here include the Critical Path Method, resource allocation, earned value analysis and various financial evaluation tests.

Delivering Successful Projects

Overall, we hope that both dossiers provide a clear and even-handed view of the theories, processes, tools and techniques which together make up project management. The material in both has been designed for study by practising and aspiring project managers, with an emphasis on encouraging the transfer of learning to the workplace.

As well as providing a wealth of information for the general reader, *Delivering Successful Projects* will support candidates working towards the NEBS Management Diploma and the Management S/NVQ at Level 4.

If you are working towards either qualification, your approved centre will provide guidance on how your study of *Delivering Successful Projects* fits in with the overall programme. Appendix 3 of this dossier contains information about the NEBS Management Diploma.

www.universal-manager.co.uk

LEARNING PROFILE

Topics included in this dossier are listed below. Use them to make a quick judgement about the level of your current knowledge and understanding, and to highlight the sections of the dossier which will be most useful to you.

KEY	Low	You have never or not recently studied this topic, nor recently applied the concepts at work.
	Mid	You have a broad understanding of the concepts or some experience of working with them, but are not confident about your current level of knowledge.
	High	You are familiar with the concepts and their theoretical underpinning. You could confidently apply the concepts in any work context.

	Low	Mid	High

(1) The Management of Projects

	Low	Mid	High
☛ The origins and development of project management as an organizational discipline	❑	❑	❑
☛ How definitions of key project management terms can vary, and the importance of establishing common terms within project teams and organizations	❑	❑	❑
☛ The range of knowledge, skills and aptitudes an effective project manager should possess	❑	❑	❑
☛ The effect that organizational structure may have on the success of projects and on the authority and effectiveness of project managers	❑	❑	❑
☛ The factors which will dictate a need for a project management approach to organizational activities.	❑	❑	❑

(2) Project Types and Cycles

	Low	Mid	High
☛ How to distinguish between different types of project and how this may influence planning and management decisions	❑	❑	❑
☛ The four stages of a basic project cycle and the activities which might occur at each stage	❑	❑	❑
☛ The purpose and application of more sophisticated project models	❑	❑	❑
☛ The structure and process contained in the PRINCE model	❑	❑	❑
☛ The arguments for and against concurrency in projects	❑	❑	❑
☛ The thrust of the 'modified design' and 'tear down the walls' philosophies.	❑	❑	❑

Delivering Successful Projects

	Low	Mid	High

(3) The Front End
- ☞ How feasibility is established at the start of projects — ❏ ❏ ❏
- ☞ How to clarify a project's scope and initial definition — ❏ ❏ ❏
- ☞ The meaning of risk management — ❏ ❏ ❏
- ☞ How a risk management process may be integrated within project management — ❏ ❏ ❏
- ☞ The content and application of a standard risk management process. — ❏ ❏ ❏

(4) The Key Players
- ☞ Techniques for organizing the project team for maximum efficiency (including the responsibility and documentation matrices) — ❏ ❏ ❏
- ☞ How creativity and conflict may be managed in the interests of project success — ❏ ❏ ❏
- ☞ How to categorize the key players in a project, and how to identify their divergent and common interests — ❏ ❏ ❏
- ☞ The importance of political awareness in a project manager — ❏ ❏ ❏
- ☞ Various political strategies and their application. — ❏ ❏ ❏

(5) Closing the Project
- ☞ The distinctions between terminated, completed and handover projects — ❏ ❏ ❏
- ☞ The factors that must be weighed when deciding whether to close a project — ❏ ❏ ❏
- ☞ A standard procedure for project closure including reporting and review — ❏ ❏ ❏
- ☞ Organizational strategies for ensuring the lessons are learned from closed projects. — ❏ ❏ ❏

www.universal-manager.co.uk

02-1 THE MANAGEMENT OF PROJECTS

02-1-1 A Brief History

Projects are as old as civilization — indeed it could be argued that the capacity to plan and execute projects is one of the defining characteristics of a civilized society. Yet in spite of the rich history of great projects in construction, exploration and military operations, it wasn't until the aftermath of World War II that the discipline we now recognize began to take shape.

Most of the tools and concepts generally bound together within the familiar project management framework, were developed between the late 1940s and early 1970s. As with so much of current management theory and practice, the initial impetus was provided by the US military and its post-war arms development programme. Pressure to produce large numbers of evermore sophisticated hardware gave rise to systems still applied by project managers today: PERT (Program Evaluation Review Technique), WBS (Work Breakdown Structure) and Earned Value are three examples which will be examined in this dossier.

The American pioneers of project management were government-funded, and motivated by four distinct but related needs:

☛ The organizational requirement to integrate multiple, diverse functions, all collaborating on huge undertakings (the forerunner was the wartime Manhattan project to build an atomic bomb)
☛ The need to estimate and control time investment (in the broad context of an 'arms race')
☛ Quality specifications
☛ The need to assess and limit uncertainty (when often they were attempting wholly original developments).

Their activity triggered private sector innovations where the motive of cost control was uppermost: Critical Path Analysis was developed within the US construction industry in the 1950s, and the concept of precedence in project planning came shortly afterwards.

The 1960s saw recognition of project management as a coherent and self-contained discipline, prompted by P O Gaddis' article in the Harvard Business Review (1959) where he picked out some issues for project managers which remain current, in particular the problem of where projects and their leaders fit within organizational structures.

The same decade witnessed what has been described as the 'paradigm of project management': the Apollo project. From the perspective of the 21st century, notwithstanding an appreciation of its technical achievement, Apollo was favoured by a set of circumstances enjoyed by very few major projects since:

- ☞ A clear, overriding objective and schedule ('a man on the moon by the end of the decade')
- ☞ Full funding approval
- ☞ Unquestioning allocation of the best available resources (human and material)
- ☞ Intense but supportive public interest.

Apollo's success brought project management techniques to greater prominence: the Project Management Institute was founded in the US during 1968; management writers began to analyse the place in business of these exciting new tools and ideas; and two important new concepts were introduced to the management vocabulary: phased project planning and the task force. In the UK, W G Downey of the Ministry of Aviation published a report on project management within the domestic defence industry, highlighting the contribution effective project management could make to cost control.

During the 1970s, particularly in the aftermath of the oil crisis, controlling costs became one of two chief concerns for those involved in managing projects — the other was controlling the project environment. Many high profile projects suffered during this decade as a result of their failure to anticipate and manage critical external factors, such as political change and public pressure — a well-known example is the Concorde development which, while it partly achieved its technical objective, did so at eight times the original budget. Even though many previous and apparently successful defence developments had been similarly wasteful of resources, from now on such excess would be unacceptable.

Despite the wealth of experience and analysis that had accumulated around project management by this stage, it was not until the late 1980s that the core techniques and ideas began to be recognized and applied widely within UK private industry: in non-technical industry sectors and within small and medium sized enterprises (SMEs). Even then, it could be argued that this wider introduction happened for 'wrong' reasons — project management was seized on especially by organizations with significant change or downsizing programmes to manage. But the 1980s also saw some wholly uncontroversial contributions to the expanding project management canon: the introduction of risk management techniques and the import from Japan of new project-centred development approaches including simultaneous engineering, partnering and what Tom Peters termed 'chunking' (pulling together specialized resources from dispersed locations). The pace-setters by now were privately owned, and at the forefront were the motor vehicle and software development companies, with their emphasis on total quality in production and fast time to market for products.

Today project management is widely practised in the developed world – whether it is widely understood is a matter of some debate. For many, the discipline is about organizing work through the use of (perhaps automated) tools such as Critical Path Analysis and Gantt charts. Others concentrate on the human side, managing the expectations of clients and stakeholders, assembling the right team and leading it effectively. Almost every recent proponent has his own pet issue, be it managing the project environment, making use of IT and ICT innovations, or building in effective risk management processes. Practical project management can encompass all of these aspects, and it is the aim of this dossier to provide a comprehensive overview of the subject.

 02-1-2 Projects, Programmes and Portfolios: What's in a Name?

Most project management courses and textbooks start with a definition of terms. There is good reason for this: experts and practitioners disagree over details. Put ten project management experts with different backgrounds into the same room, and you would wait a long while before any sensible communication developed. Terms like project or programme (program in the US) are used loosely or interchangeably, and linked concepts like portfolios, sub-projects and work packages only add to the confusion.

It's important to get these and other terms straight for several reasons:

☞   So that you will understand the rest of this dossier
☞   To enable you to make important distinctions
☞   Most significantly, at organizational and team levels, in order that those involved are speaking the same language.

So, with no apologies for starting at the obvious place, let's clarify our terms.

PAUSE TO REFLECT

What do you understand by terms like 'project', 'programme' and 'portfolio'? Is there a shared project management vocabulary in your organization?

Now read on.

Here are some textbook definitions.

Project

'. . . the allocation of resources directed toward a specific objective following a planned, organized approach.' Lientz and Rea (1998)

'All projects share one common characteristic — the projection of ideas and activities into new endeavours.' Lock (1996)

'. . . an endeavour in which human material and financial resources are organized in a novel way, to undertake a unique scope of work of given specification, within constraints of cost and time, so as to achieve unitary, beneficial change, through the delivery of quantified and qualitative objectives.' Turner (1992)

Programme (or program)

'. . . loosely coupled but tightly aligned set of projects aimed to deliver the benefits of part of a business plan or strategy.' Buttrick (1997)

'. . . programs are recurring projects. Preparing an annual review is an example of a program.' Lientz and Rea (1998)

'The co-ordinated management of a portfolio of projects which call upon the same resources.' Reiss (1996)

'. . . another example is the recycled project. This occurs when a series of similar projects is undertaken in sequence . . . an example is . . . the standard development of new variations on a product.' Lientz and Rea (1998)

Even from these few definitions, the scope for disagreement over the precise nature and composition of projects and programmes is evident — with variance occurring even within the same publication! For the purposes of this dossier, we can clearly set our own understanding of these and related terms, but it is worth stressing that project teams and organizations running projects do need to agree their own shared terminologies, and to formalize them.

For the remainder of the dossier, our intended meaning of key terms will be as follows:

A *project* is a non-routine piece of work undertaken to deliver:

- ☛ A beneficial result
- ☛ Which meets a pre-defined specification
- ☛ Within defined time and cost constraints
- ☛ And which contains an element of risk.

A *work package* is a component of the project: a piece of work contributing to project objectives, and which may be coupled with other work packages.

A *sub-project* is a work package for which responsibility has been delegated to someone other than the leader of the overall project.

A *programme* is a group of projects which together contribute to the achievement of the same strategic objective.

A *portfolio* is a group of projects managed by the same organization, team or individual, which are not necessarily aligned towards the same strategic objective.

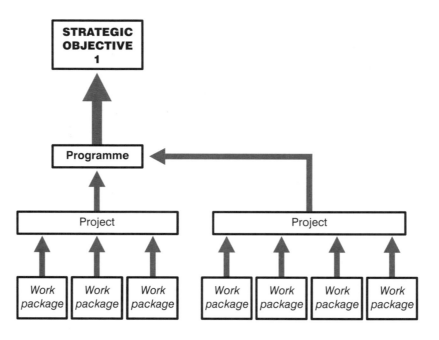

02-1-3   Characteristics of a Project Manager

The UK's Association for Project Management (APM) has identified forty key competencies required by project managers — collectively these are known as the Body of Knowledge, which sets the standard for the Certificate in Project Management. It is instructive to read through the list of competencies, and if you wish you might treat this as a self-assessment exercise to get an overview of your own current position against the national standard.

 **ACTIVITY 1**

Rate your current knowledge and experience of the following aspects of the project manager's role.

Clarification of all the terms used here can be found in the glossary at the back of this dossier.

Competency	Current knowledge			Current experience		
	High	Med.	Low	High	Med.	Low
Part 1 Project Management						
1.1 Systems Management						
1.2 Programme Management						
1.3 Project Management						
1.4 Project Life Cycle						
1.5 Project Environment						
1.6 Project Strategy						
1.7 Project Appraisal						
1.8 Project Success / Failure Criteria						
1.9 Integration						
1.10 Systems and Procedures						
1.11 Close Out						
1.12 Post Project Appraisal						
Part 2 Organization and People						
2.1 Organization Design						
2.2 Control and Co-ordination						
2.3 Communication						
2.4 Leadership						
2.5 Delegation						
2.6 Team Building						
2.7 Conflict Management						
2.8 Negotiation						
2.9 Management Development						

Competency	Current knowledge			Current experience		
	High	Med.	Low	High	Med.	Low
Part 3 Processes and Procedures						
3.1 Work Definition						
3.2 Planning						
3.3 Scheduling						
3.4 Estimating						
3.5 Cost Control						
3.6 Performance Measurement						
3.7 Risk Analysis and Measurement						
3.8 Value Management						
3.9 Change Control						
3.10 Mobilization						
Part 4 General Management						
4.1 Operations and Technical Management						
4.2 Marketing and Sales						
4.3 Finance						
4.4 Information Technology						
4.5 Law						
4.6 Procurement						
4.7 Quality						
4.8 Safety						
4.9 Industrial Relations						

Now read on.

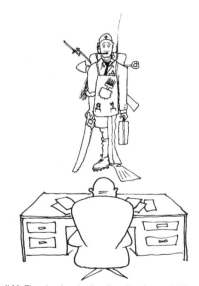

Well Mr Timmis, despite the diversity of your abilities. I'm a bit concerned about your lack of procurement experience!

Of course it is not strictly necessary for a project manager to have a mastery of all of these competencies — the extent and depth of competence required will depend chiefly on the organizational structure within which projects are managed. For instance, in a functionally structured company with occasional projects, it's likely that a project manager can call on supporting functions for the Organization and General Management areas. Whereas in a culture where 'heavyweight' status is afforded to project managers (as is the case in some Japanese motor vehicle manufacturers for example), it would not be unusual for all of these responsibilities to be project-led.

If nothing else, the Body of Knowledge convinces us that project management is a discipline for all-rounders: it isn't enough to be a brilliant specialist, an efficient administrator or an inspirational leader. Effective project managers need aptitude in all three arenas, along with a mastery of project management tools and techniques, and the ability to integrate all of these components in pursuit of the project's objectives.

The role of a manager of small or medium-sized projects is very different from the traditional line manager's role:

- ☛ The project manager tends to have a single short term purpose: the line manager's objectives will be multiple and projected onto the medium term
- ☛ A line manager must look at team performance and conduct overall, whereas a project manager is only concerned insofar as performance or conduct affect project performance
- ☛ Project managers usually need to develop close working relationships with team members; line managers (their personal style notwithstanding) tend to be more remote
- ☛ The same core differences extend to other key management actions: budgeting, control, evaluation, communication, etc.

With large projects or programmes which roll over from year to year, this distinction may be less defined. For instance, the project manager of a major construction project is unlikely to be closely involved with more than a handful of members of the project team.

02-1-4   Organizational Structure

Let's assume the senior management of a medium sized company has come to the conclusion that project management is the way ahead. They decide to start with a review of organizational structure to identify the optimum design for a project-based organization.

At present the company has a functional structure:

CHIEF EXECUTIVE

| Research & Development | Operations | Sales & Marketing | Finance & Accounts | Human Resources | Information Systems |

One option the senior management team considers is to do nothing.

PAUSE TO REFLECT

What would you see as the potential drawbacks of a functional structure in an organization where projects are managed?

Now read on.

Projects by their nature tend to require a diversity of resources — people with different skills and expertise, and sometimes a range of different material types or equipment items. The functional structure — while it offers clear communication and responsibility lines — does not contain the flexibility to integrate diverse resources successfully.

There are two further options here:

☞ *Projects are assigned to specific functions.* This is fine if the projects fit naturally within their chosen functional environments — the R&D function in our previous illustration is likely already to be managing a number of projects. Difficulties arise where the functional project leader needs to involve other functions: will Sales & Marketing give a project the priority that R&D feel it deserves? Unlikely. In addition, the functional home of the project will have its own routine work to manage alongside the project: conflict is unavoidable.

☞ *A new functional line is created, especially for projects.* To avoid the resource and priority conflicts described above, the new projects line will need to contain all the necessary functions to manage a project from start to finish. Result? Duplication of resources. The new head of projects wants his own finance team and his own marketing people.

www.universal-manager.co.uk

What if the projects line is horizontal? This creates the matrix structure.

Chief Executive's Office

Projects	Research & Development	Operations	Sales & Marketing	Finance & Accounts	Human Resources	Information Systems
Project A						
Project B						
Project C						

02-1

The influential 'In Search of Excellence' (Peters and Waterman, 1982) picks out the matrix structure as a 'favourite candidate for the wrong kind of complex response.' The chief complaint is that priorities are unclear and key resources diluted in a system designed to equalize the influence of divisions or departments, and to replace top-down bureaucracy with cross-functional contact.

With project management in mind, the matrix structure has a roughly equal distribution of benefits and drawbacks.

Pros	Cons
Powerful project leaders	Weak line managers
Flexibility to adapt to external influences	Conflict between strategic and project objectives
Avoids duplication of functional resources	Intensifies competition for the best resources
Tendency to improve resource tracking	Duplication of processes — more bureaucracy
Increased involvement of managers and staff	Delays on strategic decisions
Opportunities for multi-skilling	Reduced job stability

An alternative, advocated by Peters and Waterman (1982), is the task force or project centre. The former brings a hand-picked group together to 'storm' a specific problem — once it is solved the force will disband. The project centre — beloved of the US and Japanese motor industries — has more permanence and will tend to take on a range and a succession of strategically focussed projects. This admirable model of action-centred management, grouping specialists in an opulently resourced and highly intense environment is not a viable option for the small or medium-sized enterprise where routine cash-generating business and speculative, longer term development projects must be managed simultaneously, and by the same people.

Further down the same track is the anti-system of 'adhocracy' first identified by Mintzberg (1979). Here, formal structure is removed, roles are not defined, status is a minimal consideration and job descriptions are brief or non-existent. The advantage of this anarchic approach is thought to be in the empowerment inherent in a culture where everyone is more or less equal, and in the resulting speed at which employees feel able to take decisions and resolve problems. A genuine adhocracy relies on highly skilled people with the emotional maturity to adjust within the dynamic environment around them, and with the inclination to 'own' problems. Clearly this is not a model suited to every organization — most of us are inclined to lean on formal systems and processes and would feel lost if these were suddenly removed. Adhocracy does appear to work well in operations where the work is highly technical or creative or both: many software developers, advertising and design firms operate in a more or less adhocratic environment.

None of this however helps our senior management team: the functional structure is too inflexible, the matrix too open to conflict, the task force approach is tempting but difficult to plan for, while adhocracy is viewed as unmanageable. Fortunately, there is a middle way which is dependent upon the way projects are categorized.

We will examine various ways of categorizing projects in the next section. For now we'll assume that senior management identifies two main types of project:

☞ Internal projects which, in the main, tend to be short quality improvement initiatives with some cross-working but limited call on resources. It is decided that these can be handled within the existing functional lines.

☞ External projects which are larger and usually aimed at developing and/or delivering a product or service to the company's client base. These demand significant resourcing and cross-functional input, and often involve sub-contract or partnership arrangements. This type of project, the senior management team agrees, merits leadership from beyond the functional lines, but needs to be able to draw on functional resources. Specialists will be employed on a contract basis.

This is a hybrid design which has the advantage of building upon existing organizational structures — it could work equally well if the base structure were a matrix (the project team would still sit outside the matrix). To work really effectively, it requires a common understanding of project management terms and techniques, and integrated systems for planning, scheduling and communicating priorities.

 **ACTIVITY 2**

Assess the structure of your own organization, and evaluate the extent to which it is designed for strong project or line management.

Now read on.

 ### 02-1-5   The Need for Project Management

Project management offers a systematic approach for:

☞ Scoping the rationale for a piece of work, and the environment in which it will be undertaken
☞ Specifying what needs to be done and to what standard
☞ Planning how and when it will be done, and by whom
☞ Reviewing progress and controlling the use of resources.

Before closing this section it is important to consider exactly why an organization would need to establish such a system for the management and performance of these tasks. After all, don't many operations get along fine without formal project management processes?

The answer is yes, many do, but the world is changing and there are several significant trends which do point towards a need for systematic ways of deploying resources, analysing the environment, maximizing ideas and designs: all of which can be delivered by project management.

☞ *Globalization* affects all of us to some extent, but particularly for those firms competing directly in the global marketplace it places a premium on the ability to manage complexity (different languages and cultures) and co-ordinate dispersed operations. Neither can be accomplished without rigorous analysis, specification and planning.

☞ *Technological acceleration* has brought enormous benefits, but for organizations of all sizes there are equally significant problems: how to keep pace when new products are introduced almost at quarterly intervals, how to ensure compatibility with suppliers and partners, and how to ward off the hackers and mutant killer viruses. The clear need is for a system capable of controlling the risks and maximizing the benefits of developing technologies.

☞ *Intensifying competition.* There are few monopolies now and even in markets dominated by a few giants, there is an often bewildering choice of brands and models. The effect is that manufacturers are embroiled in a kind of 'goods race': the prize is market leadership, and the way most try to win it is by releasing more products, faster and at a lower cost. Project management techniques are required to co-ordinate across and between product ranges, and to minimize defects.

☞ To identify *empowerment* as a trend is perhaps misleading — the drive for more responsible and accountable employees at all levels of organizations seems unlikely to slow down. With increasingly educated workforces who have ever-improving access to information, self-management is probably here to stay. But empowerment needs careful management: standard processes and procedures are required to prevent autonomy turning into isolation. The structure provided by project management may not be the only solution here, but it is an effective one.

It should not be inferred from the previous paragraphs that project management is a panacea for all of the challenges facing 21st century organizations. Many other emerging practices (such as Knowledge Management or Best Practice Transfer) have been developed in response to the trends we have identified. But project management is undoubtedly an effective means by which organizations can systematically plan, control and review complex and critical activities.

www.universal-manager.co.uk

02-1

PAUSE TO REFLECT

In general, what factors would you pinpoint as indicators of a requirement for a project management system?

Now read on.

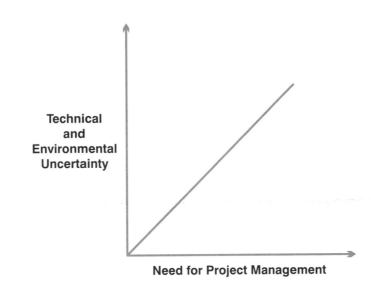

Need for Project Management

(y-axis label: **Technical and Environmental Uncertainty**)

The simple graph above illustrates the point that the extent of technical and environmental uncertainty in an endeavour, is roughly matched by the need for the application of a project management system. If you aren't clear at the outset how you are going to achieve your goal, and what influence external factors may have, it makes sense to proceed cautiously in stages, and to control the risks as tightly as possible — this is what project management does.

The same graph could have been drawn for the following factors:

☛   The extent to which different and/or dispersed teams or individuals will need to work together
☛   The size of the undertaking
☛   The complexity of the work
☛   The urgency of the deadline.

The greater any of these considerations, the greater the need for a project management system to specify, plan, co-ordinate and control the work.

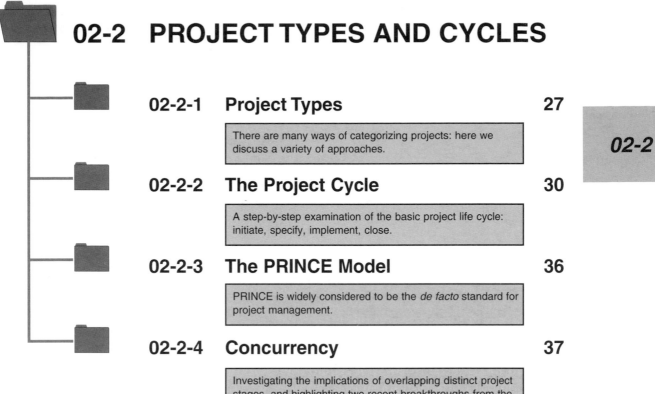

02-2

02-2   PROJECT TYPES AND CYCLES

CASE STUDY

A local government department managed a large portfolio of projects. The vast majority were short-term, taking a year or less to complete, with only one or two of a longer duration. In addition, most of the projects were fairly simple in terms of:

☞ Aims and objectives (always defined in advance)
☞ The specified end results (also defined in advance)
☞ Resourcing (budgets set in advance; one internal project manager and one or two sub-contractors per project).

Most of the projects were developmental, aimed at improving awareness and take-up of local services. Invariably the success or failure of most projects rested on the extent to which local organizations and individuals could be reached and influenced.

A decision was taken to invest in a new, sophisticated piece of project management software which was installed on all PCs. Everyone in the department received two days' training on the use of the software. This covered: how to create Gantt and PERT charts; identifying critical paths; analysing variance; modelling for various scenarios; and profiling resources. The package chosen was the most powerful then on the market, and it was agreed that it would be used for the management of all projects.

Some time after the installation and training, at the half-year departmental review, it emerged that:

☞ Project performance had not improved
☞ Most project managers felt that using the software was a time-wasting and unnecessarily complex process
☞ Despite the training most claimed not to fully understand the system
☞ As a result most had quietly returned to manual techniques.

The point of this case study is not that project management software is useless — judiciously selected, and correctly used, it can contribute a great deal to effective project management. The key point is that software is a tool, and like all tools, not appropriate to every situation. In the case outlined above, the suspicion is that for the vast majority of projects handled, a sophisticated, automated package with the full complement of 'power features', was unnecessary and unwieldy. The project managers' disenchantment probably stemmed from the 'overpromise' of many software products — project management software doesn't manage projects, it merely helps people plan and track them.

An analysis of the types of project the department dealt with would have been a sensible starting point for the identification of appropriate tools and techniques. The requirements for a three year project involving fifteen staff and eight external agencies are very different from those of a six-month project with one project manager and one consultant.

02-2-1   Project Types

In this part of the section we will survey a few of the approaches taken by project management writers to the categorization of projects.

We have already met the *internal* and *external* types of project. These are identified by Reiss (1996) in 'Programme Management Demystified'.

PAUSE TO REFLECT

Do you recall the distinction between internal and external projects?

Now read on.

Internal projects aim to introduce organizational change or improvements, whereas *external* projects deliver their end product(s) to a client or customer outside the organization.

Reiss goes on to look at some other ways of distinguishing between projects.

Physical and Non-physical

The former type has tangible outputs (cars, bridges, oil, etc.); the latter may have an intellectual end result (such as a report), a 'cyber-product' like a website or computer operating system or it may effect a change in attitude or behaviour. An advertising campaign would be one example.

Categorizing your project as physical or non-physical can be helpful in making decisions about the project team and about the nature of planning and communication that should take place. For instance, with a physical construct like a bridge, once an acceptable plan has been drawn up and circulated, the project manager's contact with sub-contractors can focus on progress: communication can therefore afford to be at reasonable intervals and according to a fixed template.

With an ambitious new website on the other hand, there will probably be a need to manage frequent communication between designer, content provider and programmer: and in the early stages, formats for communication may be fairly loose to encourage a flow of ideas and exchange of information.

Open and Closed

These are standard categories: an open project begins without a clear definition of what is going to be done and how (although deadlines and budgets may occasionally be pre-set). Closed projects start with a clear and detailed specification (the project manager knows exactly what has to be done and how).

Some writers refine the open/closed dichotomy and talk about:

☞ Semi-closed projects (what has to be done is known, but not how)
☞ Semi-open (how is known, but not what).

A more entertaining version of these definitions is provided by Eddie Obeng (quoted in Buttrick, 1997).

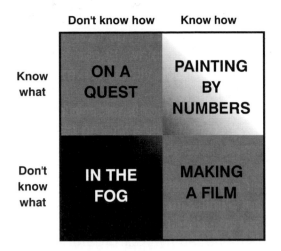

The advantages of identifying at the outset, which of these categories your project belongs to, are that:

☞   It helps to identify broadly what level of uncertainty the project is exposed to
☞   It sets the scene for how the project should be managed in the early stages (an open project for instance will probably need to be developed cautiously until aims, objectives, resourcing and methodologies become clear).

It should be evident from the last point that most projects pass through at least three of the open, semi-open, semi-closed and closed stages. For example a construction project is open until the sponsor decides what is wanted; the architect receives a brief for what is now a semi-closed project; by the time the construction company is involved, the project is in the closed category.

In one of the standard project management texts, Lock (1998) applies a completely different rationale in devising his four project categories:

☞   Civil Engineering, construction, petrochemical, mining and quarrying (high risk, capital intensive, often joint ventures)
☞   Manufacturing (mainly on-site, product-oriented and offering scope for concurrent or sequential transfer of technology and design)
☞   Management (often change or quality improvement projects)
☞   Research (high risk projects often with vague objectives; funding can be dependent upon 'political' factors).

Finally, Dr Ralph Levene (quoted by Reiss, 1998) supplies three categories which are a function of the frequency with which projects occur in an organization.

☛ *Runners* are commonly occurring projects, operated in line with standard procedures and usually offering a low risk

☛ *Repeaters* are slightly less frequent, and as a result will contain greater uncertainty

☛ *Strangers* are one-off projects with the highest risk attached.

 **ACTIVITY 3**

Select one or two of the classification systems described in this section and apply them to projects managed by your organization or department.

How helpful are the distinctions this approach encourages?

Does your organization or department apply its own categories to different types of project? If so, what are the categories and what are the practical benefits of distinguishing between projects in this way?

Now read on.

02-2-2   The Project Cycle

It will come as no surprise that there are many and various interpretations of the form that projects take. A basic project life cycle is shown on the next page. An immediate response would be that this is not in fact a natural cycle — the loop cannot be closed because this would imply a purgatorial, endless repetition of the same project. However, if we consider the project manager as a resource, freed by one project's closure to start another, the cyclical form is appropriate.

Because of its simplicity, this basic cycle does have a broad application to many different types of project, and therefore offers a useful starting point for a discussion of the key stages in the life of a project.

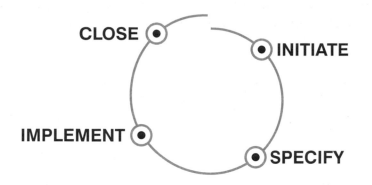

PAUSE TO REFLECT

Before reading on, think about the types of activity you would attribute to each of the four stages of this cycle.

Now read on.

Initiate

This is sometimes known as the feasibility stage — a slightly more informative term perhaps because it is here that information is gathered about the project's aims, objectives, scope, strategy and key components. An estimated timetable should be prepared and a ballpark cost calculated.

The end point of the first phase will typically be a decision on whether or not to go ahead, and this will need to be based on an assessment of:

☞ Whether the project is worth carrying out (does it contribute to strategic objectives?)
☞ Whether the project can be carried out (are sufficient and appropriate resources likely to be available?)
☞ Whether there is anything which could prevent the project achieving its aim (what are the environmental threats, what level of complexity is involved?).

The decision point at the end of the 'initiate' stage is sometimes referred to as a 'gate' which conveys reasonably well the idea that in order to proceed, an affirmative decision is needed ('unlocking' the gate).

It is possible for a project to spend years locked in the 'initiate' stage owing to a lack of political support or funding. In some organizations it is customary to distinguish between 'development opportunities' (which have not yet transferred beyond the 'initiate' stage) and projects (which have received approval for detailed planning to begin).

Specify

In physical projects, the term 'design' may be preferred to 'specify': either will do. It is at this stage that the detailed project planning takes place, resulting in various breakdowns of:

- All the work to be undertaken — known as a Work Breakdown Structure (WBS)
- (Particularly with physical projects) the desired end results — known either as a Product or Component Breakdown Structure (PBS or CBS)
- The assignment of responsibility for carrying out the work (perhaps using a matrix format)
- Resource requirements.

Individually all of these breakdowns provide vital information, but collectively they constitute a rather cumbersome planning document. This is why the data they contain is usually converted into a composite plan which may take a number of forms: Gantt charts, PERT charts and Critical Path Analyses are the most common and all three are discussed in detail in Dossier 03 *Planning and Controlling Projects*.

The 'specify' stage should also result in a project budget and schedule (prepared from a refinement of the cost and time estimates from the 'initiate' stage), and clear statements of the project's modus operandi (this may cover standard operating procedures, review points, methodologies, communication lines and other conventions).

There is a gate at the end of this stage too. By now many resources have been committed to the project but it is not too late to pull out before the stage at which greatest consumption takes place: implementation.

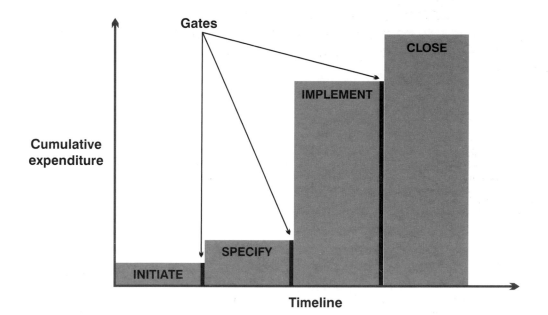

Before moving on to look at the 'implement' stage, it is worth testing our basic cycle with a commonplace example: the process of tendering and bidding for contracts. The test is this: at which stage does the tendering and bidding process occur?

The 'initiate' stage as described contains no detailed planning, only estimates and outlines. Would this level of detail be acceptable for a major project like the manufacture of an aeroplane or the construction of tunnel? The answer is no — companies tendering for even marginal involvement in this kind of project are expected to build prototypes which can cost millions and take years to complete. Of course these are mega-projects for which few companies compete, but the principle is established: the larger, more complex and more risky the project, the longer it will be before resources are fully committed.

☞ At one end of the spectrum is the 'fly before buy' approach for mega-projects, where the buyer expects a highly detailed specification and perhaps a prototype before making a decision to award the contract.

☞ At the other extreme, contracts can be awarded on the basis of an estimate subject to refinement if the proposal is successful. This approach acknowledges the problem, particularly for a small business, of committing resources to detailed planning and prototyping without a guaranteed contract.

Larger projects may need to need to go through several gates within the first two stages, during which the principal concern of decision-makers will be to receive a full analysis of the risks associated with proceeding. We look at risk assessment in the next section.

Delivering Successful Projects

Implement

The temptation is to perceive this stage as a foregone conclusion: 'just do it'! If the planning has been carried out as effectively and rigorously as it should have been, what can possibly go wrong?

Of course, it is not possible to plan for every eventuality, and implementation is often about managing the factors that weren't foreseen. It will also involve more routine management and control of work teams, budgets and physical resources. Frequent monitoring should be carried out and focussed reviews should involve all the key players in keeping the project on track.

There may be a gate at the end of the implement stage, particularly if the project's aim is to develop a new product or service. Decision-making will concern whether and how to release the new development, and may lead to refinement or scrapping the project's results altogether.

Close

Many projects fail for lack of a closure or exit strategy. Not defining this clearly (during the specify stage) can have serious consequences:

- ☞ Failure to benefit from the project's achievements
- ☞ Confusion over accountability/responsibility for the project's results
- ☞ Failure to learn from the project
- ☞ Waste of resources — an idle project team for example.

Physical projects are less susceptible to this problem than the non-physical type. With the former, once the bridge is built or the new model launched, the project has clearly ended and the main concern is re-deployment of team members and other resources. But non-physical projects, where the finished article is harder to define, may have difficulty in simply determining when the job is complete. Research or development projects may have trouble finding an owner for their end results.

02-2

 **ACTIVITY 4**

Apply our basic cycle to a project for which you have responsibility. Is it clear where the project activities fit within the cycle?

Now read on.

You may have found from the previous activity that the basic cycle illustrated is not sufficiently sophisticated to provide an accurate breakdown of the kind of project you deal with.

There are various alternative models for project breakdown — Morris (1997) provides a useful summary in 'The Management of Projects'. Among those he looks at are:

☛ The product development life cycle which incorporates research and development, as well as the growth, maturity and deterioration of the product.
☛ The 'waterfall' cycle designed specifically for software development, emphasizing iterative design, development and testing.
☛ S J Wearne's model for capital construction projects: a cycle taking in stages for study, evaluation, design, contracts, manufacture and construction, commissioning, use, maintenance and record keeping.
☛ The Pentagon's basic cycle which highlights funding approval.
☛ The 'spiral' cycle designed to show up the repetitive nature of evaluation, development and planning activities in large projects.

In your reading on project management you may also come across project models which use the term 'phase' rather than 'stage', and there are some which use both. If there is a distinction between the terms, it is not made clear in most project management literature!

The most helpful differentiation we have come across is supplied by Buttrick who:

☞ Defines a stage as a 'specific period during which work on the project takes place'

☞ While a phase is a feature of 'a project that is to be built or designed with benefits designed to arrive in different time frames. For example, major roads projects . . . introduced in phases so motorists can benefit from the first 20 miles built. Each phase is in fact a project in its own right and comprises a number of stages.'

In this dossier we consistently opt for the term 'stage'.

02-2-3   The PRINCE Model

PRINCE (Projects in Controlled Environments) is a project management method first developed by the Central Computer and Telecommunications Agency (CCTA) in 1989 as a UK Government standard for IT project management.   Since its introduction, PRINCE has become widely used in both the public and private sectors and is now considered in some quarters to be the UK's *de facto* standard for project management.

Although originally developed for the needs of IT projects, the method has recently been refined and its latest incarnation, PRINCE 2, is designed to provide a generic model for a wider audience.

PRINCE 2 is a process-based approach for project management providing a base method which can be tailored to suit projects of different scales and natures. The process model defined in PRINCE 2 introduces some concepts not met in our discussion so far of the basic 'initiate-specify-implement-close' model.

Process Model for Prince 2

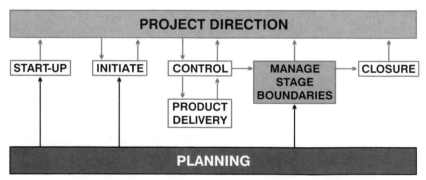

Among the key variations from our basic model are:

☞ Separation of the task of managing transition between stages — this can be akin to bridging a chasm, particularly where separate organizations are responsible at adjacent stages

☞ The view of planning as a continuous activity spanning the entire project. Planning here is product-based, which means that project plans focus on delivering results and are not simply about planning when project activities will be carried out

☞ The recognition that the directorial role in a project requires continued involvement throughout a project's life and does not end with the approval of funding.

02-2

Priority is afforded by the PRINCE 2 model to the establishment of a 'business case' for a project — this describes the organization's justification, commitment and rationale for the project's deliverables. The business case is regularly reviewed during the project to ensure that strategic objectives, which may be subject to change during the project lifecycle, are still being met.

02-2-4 Concurrency

Since the late 1960s, project management writers and practitioners have conducted an occasionally heated debate over the pros and cons of concurrency. The essential concept is simple and seductive: instead of waiting until the whole product is designed before building it, why not begin construction and testing of key components as their design is completed. This enables some design and some construction to be carried out simultaneously, shortening the development time, and increasing the speed with which products can be released onto the market. The concept will transfer to most types of project but is most at home within the sphere of product development.

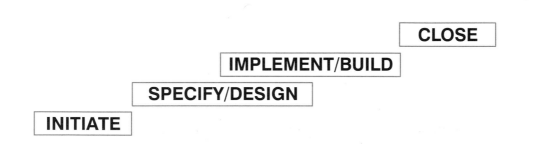

 **ACTIVITY 5**

In your own organization, what objections can you see being raised against the idea of concurrent development?

Compare your suggestions with our commentary in Appendix 1.

Concurrency had its heyday in the late 1980s and early 1990s with the advent of 'lean thinking', recognized in the seminal motor industry-based text by Womack and Ross (1990), 'The Machine that Changed the World'. The essence of lean thinking was that greater efficiency and market share could be achieved by companies (primarily manufacturers) who stripped away the excess people, time and costs from their operations. Key principles were:

☞ Cross functional teams led by heavyweight project managers
☞ Rapid replacement of models
☞ Overlapping work stages (i.e. concurrency).

But lean thinking has fallen out of favour, for reasons too many and diverse to analyse here. For project management the important thing about lean thinking's demise is the set of ideas that have supplanted it.

The originators of lean thinking were the large Japanese motor manufacturers, Toyota and Honda, but they do things differently now. According to Cusumano and Nobeoka (1998), the guiding principles now are:

☞ Take longer over planning and design
☞ Concentrate on innovative designs
☞ Avoid low value features
☞ Share common components between different models.

These ideas are applicable in most environments where programme or portfolio management goes on: it is the sharing of components that is key. Where there is a strategic overview of various projects in a programme or portfolio, and one which grasps the common areas and links between them, efficient management of resources should result. Couple this with an emphasis on excellent design and you get not only greater efficiency and increased market share, but also a higher quality in the end products.

A further riposte to concurrency came from the US motor industry. Reiss (1998) describes the 'tear down the walls' culture engineered at Chrysler which resulted in the Viper model and which broke all previous records for time to market. Tearing down the walls meant putting the designers and engineers in the same room and forcing them to work together.

02-2

These two relatively new management ideas ('modified design' and 'tear down the walls') have some relevance for just about any industry sector: in software development, designers must work closely with programmers; NHS Trusts can achieve greater purchasing power by co-ordinating resource needs analysis among different Directorates; publishers can save on design, print and authoring costs if they identify the common features within a range before commissioning.

02-3 THE FRONT END

02-3

02-3   THE FRONT END

02-3-1   Establishing Feasibility

Every project springs from an identified need: this supplies its driving purpose. How far a project goes towards fulfilling its purpose will depend on the extent to which the identified need can feasibly be met. The 'initiate' and 'specify' stages described in the previous section are concerned with establishing a project's feasibility, removing as much risk as possible from the operation before the major commitment of resources occurs.

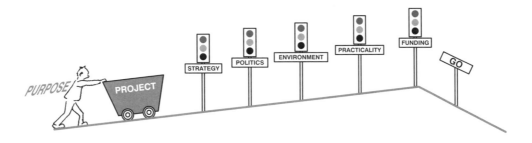

Our illustration shows the most significant 'checkpoints' a project must negotiate to establish its feasibility.

- ☞ *Strategy*. A project which doesn't contribute to the strategic goals of both the sponsor and the manager is hardly worthy of consideration. When assessing the merits of competing project ideas, the strategic contribution to be made by each should be the prime criterion.
- ☞ *Politics* can thwart a project which in all other respects is perfectly feasible. We refer here to internal politics, particularly within the sponsoring organization or unit. A project manager needs to be adept at identifying the interests of various key players, and at adopting strategies calculated to appeal to these (even when they appear to conflict).
- ☞ The *environmental* factors affecting project success might include economic conditions, competitive projects, public opinion, technological developments, etc. Even with a small, apparently self-contained project the impact of external factors cannot be played down — for instance, what price an ISO9000-driven quality improvement initiative when the competition has switched attention to the Business Excellence Model?
- ☞ *Practicality* comprises a number of subsidiary concerns: whether the deadline is realistic; whether the requisite expertise and skills are available; whether the material and technical resources can be obtained, and so on.
- ☞ *Funding* approval is not always the last checkpoint in line, but it is good practice not to make a full resource commitment until all of the other stages have been passed.

 **ACTIVITY 6**

What form do these checkpoints take in the projects you manage?

02-3

What systems are in place to help negotiate them?

Now read on.

A common tool used to gather and present the information needed to initiate a project is a *scoping brief*. This is a format with the dual purpose of helping the project initiator (who need not necessarily be the same person as the project's manager) to:

☞ Analyse *what* the project is trying to do, *who* for, *why* and *how*
☞ Present that information to decision-makers and others involved in starting the project.

A basic outline of a scoping brief is supplied on the next page. We have filled it in as if it were being used to plan the development of this dossier.

Purpose (Why?)	People (Who?)
To establish the sponsors as suppliers of unique and high quality management materials	*For:* Experienced and aspiring middle managers NEBS Management Diploma candidates S/NVQ Level 4 Management candidates *Interested parties:* Suppliers of management training and development *Sponsors* NEBS Management Scitech-DIOL
End result (What?) A paper-based dossier on Project Management	**Standards (How?)** By March 31st 2000 Tested with pilot centres and a subject expert Within budget Providing a comprehensive and authoritative survey of current project management theory and practice Clearly and attractively designed and laid out Adding to the study and practice of project management

PAUSE TO REFLECT

In your judgement, are there any important considerations missing from this definition of project scope?

Now read on.

Although it may appear simple, it would be a mistake to underestimate the quality of information demanded by the above format.

☞   The purpose, for instance, is concerned with *why* we should undertake this project — this is a strategic question, distinct from project objectives or goals which will state *what* is to be achieved.

☞   The people identified are end users (customers); stakeholders (anyone who may have an interest in the project or its outcomes); and the sponsor or client (who bankrolls the project). Identifying these parties is the first step in analysing the political and environmental factors which might have an impact on the project.

☞   The end result should offer a clear statement of what the project will produce, but this need not be limited to physical products — attitude shifts or raised awareness are valid end results (provided there is a means of measuring them).

☞   Standards are success indicators — the criteria that a successful project will fulfil. Time, budget and quality are the prime considerations, but standards may be set which go beyond the life of the project and focus on the take-up or sustainability of the end results.

02-3

There are however, a number of additional factors which might be included in the scoping brief as an aid to decision-making and planning.

☞   Distinct from the purpose, project objectives may be established

☞   In the people box, we might add the category of 'participants' — those who will be involved in carrying out the project

☞   A broad assessment might be made of environmental conditions: internal factors might include the organization's track record, activities and interests linked to the proposed project, opportunities for resource sharing or maximization; external factors could take in a market analysis, regulation changes, economic conditions or developments in technology

☞   It can be useful to begin to break down the project, identifying its major parts and an outline schedule for carrying them out

☞   Linked to the breakdown would be a ballpark estimate of costs and resource needs.

CASE STUDY

The construction of the Channel Tunnel is one of the best known projects of recent years. The idea became a real possibility in 1955, but it was not until 1987 that plans were officially sanctioned by both the French and UK governments. The contract was for bored twin rail tunnels with a vehicle shuttle, and was won by the Channel Tunnel Group (CTG), comprising Eurotunnel (the group's owners) and Transmanche-Link (the contractors). Associated development was agreed to establish high quality rail and road links on both sides of the channel.

Its physical legacy aside, the project will perhaps be best remembered for the financial wrangling that surrounded it from the go-ahead to completion in 1994. It was a rare example of what has been termed a 'BOO(T)' project. This stands for 'Build – Own – Operate – (Transfer). Typically a BOO(T) project will have a public sector client but will be financed mainly or entirely by the private sector — this means that the contractor (rather than the client) takes on financing and ownership of the finished result, perhaps with the medium term aim of selling or transferring it back into the public domain.

This modification of the usual client-project manager relationship was further complicated in the Channel Tunnel project by the fact that CTG contributed only a fraction of the required capital (at the start) and relied on a phased sale of share options to raise remaining funds. The CTG board was split between banks and contractors — a clash of interests was inevitable. There were good reasons for the approach CTG took to raising finance — investors were unlikely to commit to the project in the early stages when the risks were highest. But it had dire consequences for the management of the project: design was continually constrained by the need to build something — anything — to sway the markets, and this resulted in important oversights which delayed completion by over a year and doubled initial cost forecasts.

 **ACTIVITY 7**

From this brief account, and from your own knowledge of the Channel Tunnel project, construct an initial scoping brief. You may choose whichever project definitions you think appropriate — the purpose of this exercise is to practise applying them to a live project.

Compare your ideas with ours in the commentary in Appendix 1.

02-3

 ## 02-3-2 Risk Management

Risk is uncertainty — risk management involves controlling the risk inherent in work activities. By many definitions, projects necessarily contain a degree of risk — they are non-routine, new endeavours — and it is the role of the project manager to define, contain and occasionally to capitalize on that risk. The word 'capitalize' may appear perverse, but it is important to recognize that risk is not always a negative phenomenon. For instance, the possibility that a construction project might finish ahead of schedule should be considered a risk, and a double-sided one:

☞ The *upside* risk could be that early completion will result in bonuses paid by a satisfied client
☞ The *downside* risk might reside in the potential for resources committed to the project to become idle, and not easy to re-deploy.

We have already discussed one widely applied technique for controlling project risk: delaying commitment of resources until a full study of feasibility has been carried out. In general, the definition of resource outlay and project risk should sharpen the further a project progresses, so that by the time implementation is approved, only Acts of God can prevent success!

But there are more complex and rigorous approaches which are increasingly being applied to capital cost projects and other high value undertakings containing a high degree of uncertainty. These are known as Risk Management Processes (RMPs) and a useful example was devised by the Ministry of Defence in 1991. It consists of five distinct stages which are set out below in relation to our four standard project stages:

Project Stages　　**Risk Management Stages**

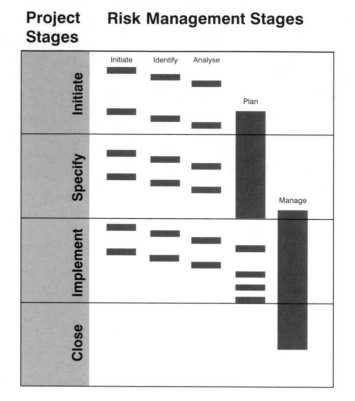

The five stages in the MOD process can be defined as follows:

☞ *Initiation* should not be seen purely as a start-up activity. It involves consolidating all project information available, identifying gaps and filling them - these are activities likely to be repeated as more information about the project is gathered. In a sense, this stage provides an assessment of the rigour and comprehensiveness with which project management techniques are being applied.

☞ The *identification* stage makes specific the nature of the risks to which a project may be exposed. These may be identified by reference to records, via team activities such as brainstorming sessions, and by using checklists. The named risks are then classified, perhaps in terms of their scale, whether they are positive or negative, or in terms of the response they call for.

This stage should provide the project team with a clear understanding of the risks facing their project and a system for classifying risks and their associated response options. Again, this stage should not be viewed as a one-off although the bulk of the work may be carried out in one hit — the nature of risk management is continuously to review and refine.

☛ The *analysis* stage contains two interdependent activities: clarification of responsibility and accountability for identified risks, and quantification of risks in terms of their significance for the project. The outcome of analysis should be a refined system for diagnosing and responding to risks, in accordance with their significance. A temptation can be to devise complex risk rating systems when in reality, the project manager and sponsor are primarily concerned with highlighting potential 'show-stoppers'.

☛ *Planning* builds on all the foregoing work to contribute to the production of a project plan (or 'base' plan) containing all the necessary detail for implementation (e.g. timing, precedence, resourcing, responsibility, etc.). This integration with 'mainstream' project management is important: risk management should not be seen as an adjunct to the practical business of managing the project. The project manager should 'own' the risk management process, and view it as essential component of preparation and planning.

Having said that, the RMP planning stage goes beyond what is usually seen as the base planning remit, and will also result in risk assessments for those aspects of the plan where risk has been identified: these will detail the significance of the risk and its associated response options. Finally the planning stage will generate contingency plans, with a similar coverage to the base plan.

☛ *Management* is an ongoing stage that starts with the implementation of the project, and involves monitoring project progress in relation to the base plan and (where applied) risk management plans. Management of the RMP may involve identifying a need to review and refine existing plans.

02-3

A more intricate, nine-stage process for risk management was devised by Chris Chapman for the Association for Project Management — the major difference between this and the MOD version is that analysis is broken up into four separate stages (structure, ownership, estimate and evaluate). The process is described in detail in 'Project Risk Management' by Chapman and Ward (1998), recommended to anyone looking for an in-depth analysis of the principles and practices of risk management.

02-4 THE KEY PLAYERS

02-4

02-4   THE KEY PLAYERS

02-4-1   Project Teams

Nowadays it is a commonplace to come across a Chief Executive or MD declaring: 'In this business, it's the people that make a difference.' This attitude has been slow to permeate the confines of project management — perhaps because such great emphasis is placed in most textbooks and training programmes on the processes of scoping, planning, risk assessment, etc. Yet, it is clear that the nature of most projects places a premium on having the right people, working in the right environment, such that the quality of the relationships between them is conducive to excellent performance.

 **ACTIVITY 8**

Think about a project you have been involved in recently — what 'people factors' most significantly affected its management and outcomes?

Now read on.

We know that, in general, projects are non-routine endeavours, often containing a degree of risk and complexity, and often subject to time and budget constraints. The clear implications are that project people should be capable of managing or working with uncertainty, not averse to working under pressure, and competent at what they do (project schedules are rarely forgiving of wasted effort or serious errors).

It is crucial that a common purpose and language are shared by project participants — it is the job of the project manager to establish and communicate these at an early stage. Different contributors will often work on different stages of the project, and it is not always necessary for them to have sight of the whole plan. But unless they are made aware of the plan's unifying features (the overall objectives, target audience, strategy and standards, etc.), their chances of making a suitable contribution that is fit for purpose will be impaired.

A simple tool commonly used to clarify the roles of individual contributors to a project is the *responsibility matrix*, illustrated below by way of a simple project.

Responsibility Matrix

PROJECT: Re-organize Stock Room

WHAT / WHO	Refine product range	Identify surplus stock	Re-design storage	Revise stock procedures	Re-organize storage
Mills	✔	✔			
Sreenevasan		✔	✔	✔	✔
Allan	✔				✔
Cullpepper				✔	✔
Ryan			✔		✔
Ghosh		✔		✔	✔

02-4

This format shows the assignment of responsibilities on a project, and conversely, the human resources committed to each key task or work package. Linkages or matters of precedence are not made clear, and in a complex project it would not be reasonable to expect participants to be able to infer dependencies and links from a basic responsibility matrix.

As an optional adjunct to the responsibility matrix, some organizations like to issue briefing or assignment documents to each contributor (these should be variations on a standard template). These tend to be less useful to the project manager in terms of the overview they provide, but can be essential for team members and sub-contractors. Key information to get across will include:

☛ Appropriate elements from the project's overall definition — it is usually good practice for team members to know the overall direction, timetable and standards for the project

☛ A description of the task to be carried out

☛ Timescales (the detail here will vary: a simple deadline may suffice, but it may be necessary to outline milestones or to fix earliest and latest start and finish times for the activity)

☛ Standards to be applied in assessing performance on this activity

☛ Significant links with other activities or other contributors to this activity

☛ Availability of resources and support for completion of the activity.

Another possible adjunct to the responsibility matrix is the *documentation matrix,* illustrated below. This is another tool to help the project manager plan and convey individual and grouped contributions to the project, and to ensure that contributors get the information they need to fulfil their responsibilities.

Documentation Matrix

PROJECT: Re-organize Stock Room

WHAT / WHO	Price list	Stock list	Stock room layout	Stock procedures
Mills	✔	✔		✔
Sreenevasan		✔	✔	✔
Allan	✔		✔	✔
Cullpepper			✔	✔
Ryan			✔	✔
Ghosh			✔	✔

02-4-2   Creativity and Conflict

There is a tendency towards autonomous units or empowered teams in project management (whether external sub-contractors or internal work teams). Typically, once the project leader or co-ordinator has recruited and briefed contributors, management thereafter will be via a schedule of review points — and where the style is for 'management by exception', this allows vast scope for ignorance of the totality of contributor activities on the part of the project manager. It is therefore all the more critical for all participants to be working on a current, common project plan which is clear about the unifying and immutable features of the project — scope for creativity is thus contained within defined limits.

Many of the recent developments in team working (self-managed teams, 'tear down the walls', creative conflict, etc.) are particularly suited to project teams. The unique challenges of moulding an effective unit from various contributors – likely to be dispersed in location, and divergent in terms of background, specialism and culture — is worthy of serious study. John Whatmore (1999) has some interesting things to say about how effective leaders extract maximum creativity from their teams. One tactic he describes is the deliberate use of tension to generate a sense of urgency and unlock creative solutions:

> *'Some leaders orchestrate (or perhaps improvise with) tensions in ways which they believe will bring the best out of individuals and the team — by making and using situations and opportunities for things to happen, where metaphor and tension will be at their most stimulating, even to the point of potential breakdown.' John Whatmore, 1999.*

CASE STUDY

(1) The theory

A government department commissioned a design company to create its website — the requirement was for an ambitious site which would not only provide a public information service, but also a series of on-line learning programmes aimed primarily at businesses.

After the initial scoping sessions, it was decided that in addition to the design and in-house contract management functions, the project would also need:

- A content provider: two department staff were given two months to generate the necessary content
- A technical function: to support the designers with programming for the website, and to provide maintenance once it was up and running
- Representation from those sections within the department with an interest in the site's content.

The PRINCE 2 process model was adapted to come up with an outline plan for development of the on-line learning part of the site:

On-line Learning Development Plan

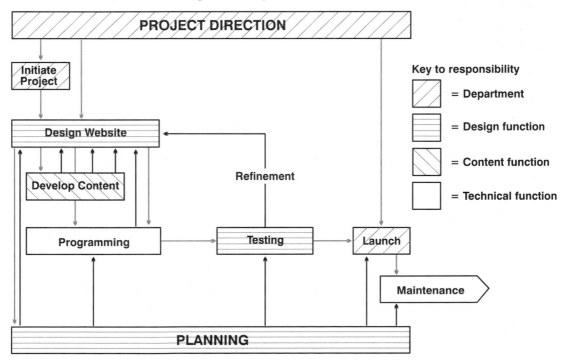

Although time was tight, it can be seen from the outline plan that testing was considered not to be viable until the complete site was up and running. However, it was felt that aspects of design, content provision and programming could happen concurrently:

- ☞ The site architecture would be designed first
- ☞ The content team would provide their material in three stages, so that the design team could make an early start on shaping the content
- ☞ As soon as a section of the site had been written and designed, it would be passed to the programming team.

(2) In practice

The project appeared to be running smoothly until the point where the programming team posted the first section of content. General reaction was unfavourable: it looked dull, there was far too much text, the content was unfocussed, and so on. Stung by this criticism, the design team blamed the content providers for churning out reams of boring and impenetrable copy. The content team (whose two months were almost up) responded in kind, averring that surely it was the designers' job to turn it into engaging, attractive on-line material. (The programmers wisely kept out of it.)

A contingency plan was quickly formulated and implemented. The content team's secondment was extended by a month. A distance learning consultant was hired and the plan was for three creative sessions to be held (one per section of content), involving all project contributors, with the objective of turning the reams of impenetrable copy into effective learning material for the internet.

There was a palpable tension at the first session: the mutual mistrust between the suited content providers and the trainer-wearing designers was unmistakable. Although some excellent ideas were generated, the lead designer did not feel that they had hit upon a truly creative treatment of the first section of content. For him, the most positive outcome from the meeting was that, for the first time, the design team had an understanding of the messages they needed to convey.

In concluding the first session, the lead designer proposed that:

- ☞ They continue with sessions two and three as scheduled, but that the focus should be on 'unpicking' the content to identify key messages
- ☞ The design team would go away after each meeting and hold internal brainstorming sessions to generate appropriate design ideas.

Relieved that things were taking a positive turn, the departmental project manager agreed to this proposal.

www.universal-manager.co.uk

(3) The outcome

By the time the website was launched, the project had overrun by three months and was about 30% over-budget. However, the design of the site was widely considered to be excellent: attractive and unusual. The on-line learning programmes were also considered a success in terms of their exciting use of visual themes and images, and their use of interactive learning features.

Several dissenting voices from within the department pointed out that the structure of the programmes was confusing and that often there was no clear connection between the text and the images on screen. Over time these criticisms were borne out by feedback from users: most liked the site but were unsure what they were supposed to gain from the on-line learning programmes.

 PAUSE TO REFLECT

Consider the team composition and structure employed for this project. How do you feel they could have been improved upon?

Now read on.

It would be fair to say that our case study illustrates unproductive conflict within a project team. The isolation of key project functions and the tension this fostered (particularly between design and content providers) contributed significantly to the project's overrun and overspend. It is significant that the attractiveness of the end product helped to hide the fact that the on-line learning materials were not especially effective.

Any project which brings together different groups, with different interests and from different cultural backgrounds, will have to incorporate a strategy for managing the resulting conflict. The project in our case study might have been more genuinely successful if:

☞ Either the department had contracted with an organization containing as many of the required specialisms as possible — it should have been possible to find a company with a better grasp of the subject matter and with a track record in developing on-line learning

☞ Or the different work teams had been brought together at an early stage to thrash out the issues (partly) addressed in the hastily convened creative sessions. Early exposure to each other's working styles and requirements, at a stage in the project where no serious work had been done and therefore no blame would be apportioned, might have resulted in the formation of a dynamic work team. At worst it would have given the project manager an early warning of the divergent approaches within the team.

02-4-3   Influencers and Decision-makers

The project team aside, there are numerous other key players who contribute to project success or failure.

PAUSE TO REFLECT

To test your recall, without looking back, see if you can define the following players in terms of their interest in a project:

Stakeholder

Client or sponsor

End user

Now read on.

A project's most influential figure is usually its **client** or **sponsor** — the person or organization that finances the work. A sponsor's main interest should provide the project with its purpose: if an advertising firm's client wishes to sell more cigarettes to the youth market, that is the purpose of the campaign irrespective of the views of the project team; a manufacturer's purpose in developing a new model will be to increase market share, not necessarily to produce a more technically refined model (which may interest the project team).

But these two examples give us an inkling that the sponsor's motivation can be complex:

02-4

- The advertising firm's client will not want the project purpose to be transparent, and it may therefore be part of the campaign's strategy to disguise the client's intentions
- The manufacturer will be aware that competitors are also likely to be developing new models to increase their own market share: so the project may have the added requirements of developing the new model in record time, and ensuring that the end product is unique and of a high quality.

Additional requirements like these will often be assigned to the project's *standards*.

The role of the client will involve paying for the project; communicating what the project should set out to achieve; agreeing the project definition and perhaps the detailed base plan; allocating resources; contributing to evaluation, review or testing of the project's deliverables; approving the deliverables.

The client will expect a competent project manager and team working to an agreed plan to produce the best possible output. Clear, timely and honest progress reports will be essential, conveying information critical to the achievement of the project's purpose, objectives and standards.

Whoever makes use of the end product of a project is an **end user**. A car driver is the end user of both the project to develop the car s/he is driving and the project to 'improve' the road s/he is driving on — if either of these end products is faulty, s/he may end up the end user of services supplied by the nearest hospital or by an anger counsellor!

The art of defining end user interest in a project is the essence of marketing, and as such is not within the scope of this dossier. However, in relation to projects, three points should be made:

☛ Projects which do not define who their end users are and what they want have a slim chance of success

☛ There is a definable strand within marketing and promotion which assumes that end users are as interested in the process as the product it delivers. Quality marks, 'ice brewing' techniques, and cosmetics advertisements which talk about 'hypo-allergenic' properties are proof of this (the last two may also be proof of the gullibility which some companies ascribe to their end users!)

☛ Organizations with a genuine interest in meeting the needs of their end users involve them in specification and testing processes so that the end product can be released with reasonable confidence.

These points are of particular relevance where the project involves development of a physical or intangible product which will be transferred somewhere else during the 'operational stage' (e.g. a new car or qualification). In this type of project the initial recipient (e.g. the operations team who will fabricate the car, or the institutions which will deliver the new qualification) should be treated as an end user.

A project's **stakeholders** may have a wide diversity of interests — some of which may be mutually exclusive. The trick for project managers is to identify the most influential stakeholders, and address their requirements first.

www.universal-manager.co.uk

Here are some common examples of stakeholders and their interests:

☞ The senior management team (SMT). In a relationship where the client is external to the organization managing a project, the SMT has control of the project's life support. Senior management will decide whether and when a project should proceed or stop, and which internal resources should be committed to it. A supportive SMT may contribute to strategic and even tactical decision-making concerning an approved project, but the overriding concern will be ensuring efficient performance, which contributes to organizational objectives.

☞ External relations. These are individuals or bodies with some connection to the project's end user. They may be literally related to the end user (for instance the parents of a college student have a natural interest in the education their child receives); or the end product of a project may influence their own service to the end user (the college has a stake in the quality of the learning materials used by the student).

☞ Internal relations. These tend to be other departments or colleagues affected by the project's process or outcomes. A departmental manager who has to release staff to a project team is a stakeholder; so is a bank branch which is next in line to implement a new process being piloted at head office.

02-4

Identifying the connections to and between stakeholders, and defining their interests, can be a complex and dispiriting business. For the exercise to be useful, sensible limits must be applied — after all, in a global economy it is possible to argue that the Taiwan government is a stakeholder in a project to review the inventory of a toy store in Leamington Spa!

Buttrick has some practical advice on what he calls 'stakeholder communication planning and tracking'. His definition of stakeholders is somewhat at odds with the one given here (he includes for instance 'users of new systems' – we would consider these to be end users, unless the new systems were a by-product of a project), but he does supply four categories of stakeholder which may be useful:

☞ *Decision-maker:* someone required to make a decision affecting the project

☞ *Influencer:* will have influence over the project and/or decision-makers

☞ *Player:* contributes to project, perhaps by providing resources or facilities; may also be involved in testing or review processes

☞ *Consenter:* can grant or withhold consent required for the project to succeed: an example might be an account manager who consents to a product pilot involving his customers.

02-4-4　Managing Relationships

Any project with a separate client and project manager will have a political aspect. Add various stakeholders to the mix, a few different contacts within the client organization and a layered project team — the result will be a complex political situation. High profile projects which are publicly funded are the most intensely political in nature, but most projects contain a tangle of interests, priorities and relationships ready to ensnare the unwary project manager.

 **ACTIVITY 9**

With your own workplace in mind, what do you think might be the consequences for project managers who, unconsciously or not, ignore the political dimension?

Compare your response with our commentary in Appendix 1.

The point is clearly made: however uncomfortable they may sometimes feel about it, for their projects to proceed serenely through all stages, and to receive the support, resourcing and recognition so crucial to success, project managers must be appreciative of the political environment and capable of acting appropriately within it.

Political project management begins with a grasp of the differing interests and influences affecting a project. Intuition may not be enough, particularly with large and complex projects, and it is often advisable at an early stage to survey key players to define:

- ☛ Their individual interests
- ☛ Shared and conflicting interests
- ☛ The extent of their potential to influence the project.

In effect, this amounts to political risk management and it should be followed through to the point where there is a clear strategy for addressing political threats and opportunities that may present themselves. In practical terms the strategy may translate into decisions about:

02-4

- ☛ Who needs to be involved in consultation, review or testing activities
- ☛ Who needs to be kept informed of project progress
- ☛ What level of detail different parties will require
- ☛ What specific aspects of the project are most important to each player.

For instance, it would not be unusual to have three or more different versions of the same project report — customized to suit the differing needs of, say, the client, the project team and major stakeholders. Many project management software programmes have the capacity to 'filter' data, so that critical paths or resource charts can be manipulated to present pre-limited information. Our illustration on the following page shows an example of filtered data concerning staff allocation to a project.

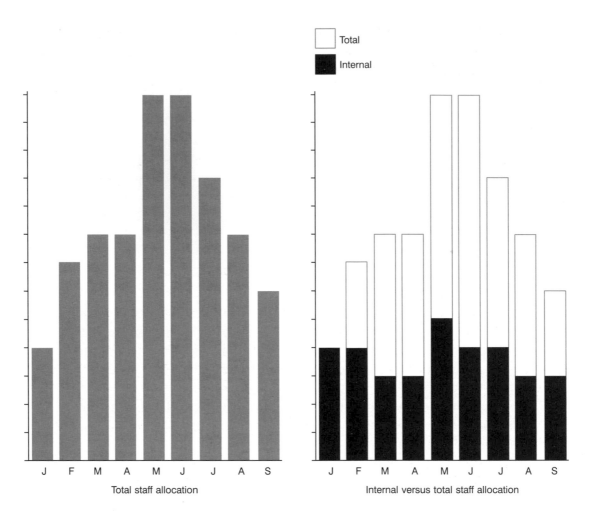

Total

Internal

Total staff allocation

Internal versus total staff allocation

But politics in project management is about more than the 'spin' applied to information. There are cultural aspects too.

☞ **CASE STUDY**

Mornings at the Grays fabrication unit of a large construction firm are kicked off by a short, 'standing session' — this is the only management meeting the MD will permit, and it has a clearly defined structure and style:

☞ The session must last no more than an hour
☞ No paper is brought in, and the session 'outcomes' are written up on a whiteboard in the main office
☞ Every project manager must attend
☞ Participants must stand for the duration of the meeting
☞ Shirt sleeve order is prescribed.

The purpose of each morning's standing session is to review progress on the unit's total work programme (which can contain up to sixteen projects at any given time), and the focus tends to be on critical problems. Each project manager in turn is invited to give a verbal update, reporting on how current problems are being addressed and identifying any emerging difficulties.

The MD's style at these meetings is challenging and searching, bordering on the abrasive. Project managers reporting, for instance, on fabrication delays or mistakes are often asked 'How does that make you feel?' The expectation is that they will go out and ensure the culprits know exactly how they feel!

The standing sessions are part of a deliberate strategy to foster an autocratic culture, where the MD and his management team are 'on top of everything', and where staff and sub-contractors are keenly aware of the consequences of under-performing.

02-4

In this environment, politically successful project managers are those who:

☞ Report fewest problems
☞ Are concise and business-like in their reporting and responses to the MD's questions
☞ Are seen to 'jump on' under-performers straightaway
☞ Are unfazed by criticism and continual challenge from the MD.

Kliem and Ludin pay particular attention to the political factor in 'The People Side of Project Management'. While admitting that some of the tactics they describe are ethically dubious, they contend that 'in order to survive [project managers] . . . may have to use the tools of the devil to defeat him.' We will end our discussion of the political side of project management with a summary of some of the strategies mentioned by Kliem and Ludin (1992):

☞ *Divide and conquer.* This strategy is effective for heading off a challenge (probably from within the project team) to the project manager's authority. The idea is to assign tasks within the project team which will create dependencies between team members — in theory difficult personalities are thus too busy responding to peer requirements to create problems. The approach may also be appropriate when there are conflicting interests within a client organization — the astute project manager is often adept at playing one party against another.  Of course, the inherent danger with 'divide and conquer' tactics is that the divided parties will establish common interests and unite against the would-be conqueror.

☞ *Co-option.* Essentially, co-option means striking a bargain with a potential source of opposition. For instance, the project manager may persuade a key stakeholder with some antipathy to the project to co-operate in return for a specific concession (perhaps greater involvement in the project, or even a paid contract). Co-option need not be a particularly sinister tactic, but if the object's opposition is strong enough, an unwary (or desperate) project manager may be tempted to offer an inducement he cannot afford.

☞ *Alliance building.* Similar to co-option, except that relationships are established with friends rather than enemies. The trick here is to make profitable alliances — often this means establishing mutually beneficial relationships with parties of sufficient stature or influence that the very association will reflect well on your own activities. The key example given by Kliem and Ludin is of an alliance between project managers which might extend to resource sharing for example.

☞ *Power-brokering.* With this strategy, the project manager acts as mediator between warring factions. It is not uncommon for project managers to be called upon to resolve conflict between key players (among stakeholders, within the client organization, etc.), and the aim should always be to find a resolution which benefits the project, or at least avoids problems. Power-brokering, however, is more opportunistic — the political project manager may choose to intervene in  disputes which do not directly affect his project, if he sees some capital in being seen as the 'peacemaker'.

☞ *Spread responsibility.* This strategy might be termed 'empowerment' or 'involvement', but these two terms have less pejorative connotations and purer motives. The project manager who fears failure, may choose to delegate authority within the team (or spread responsibility among other projects) as a shield to deflect blame. In practical terms this may involve sharing decision-making or electing to share significant resources with other projects. Applied without cynical motives, spreading responsibility for project deliverables can have the effect of motivating project contributors and ensuring that those most competent have direct influence over progress — but the project manager must remain, and be seen to remain, accountable and in overall control.

☞ *Scapegoating.* An all too familiar tactic — blaming convenient others for problems or failures in an attempt to absolve yourself from any responsibility. Of course, it is often the case that others **are** responsible for problems, but scapegoating tends to happen after the event and implies no attempt to work with others to resolve difficult situations.

☞ *Filibustering.* Beloved of parliamentarians, filibustering is a delaying tactic where the project manager's energies will be devoted to finding excuses and methods for delaying progress until the objective is achieved. There may be many reasons for wishing to delay a project: perhaps the client has insisted on starting even though the principal technology is not yet available, perhaps full funding has not yet been agreed, or there may be a key resource which is tied up until some time into the project's original schedule. Filibustering is a dangerous game, particularly if the delay threatens project viability or if the real reason for delaying is not one the project manager can declare.

02-4

☞ *Sacrificing the future for the present.* Also known as going for the 'quick fix'. This familiar strategy usually involves compromising on project quality or resourcing in order to meet the schedule. It is perhaps the chief reason for project failure, particularly prevalent at design and planning stages, where adequate time, rigour and expertise are often sacrificed to get the project moving. Political project managers are hyper-aware of the client's expectation of quick, visible results and may consider it expedient to bring forward project activities — often the intended effect is actually to protect the future (perhaps further funding or firm commitment depend upon early client satisfaction) but the real effect may be to comprise the overall integrity of project design or implementation.

You did repair that break properly, didn't you?

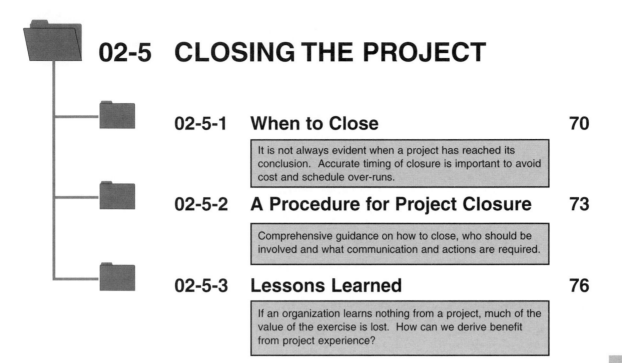

02-5 CLOSING THE PROJECT

02-5-1 When to Close   70

> It is not always evident when a project has reached its conclusion. Accurate timing of closure is important to avoid cost and schedule over-runs.

02-5-2 A Procedure for Project Closure   73

> Comprehensive guidance on how to close, who should be involved and what communication and actions are required.

02-5-3 Lessons Learned   76

> If an organization learns nothing from a project, much of the value of the exercise is lost. How can we derive benefit from project experience?

02-5

02-5 CLOSING THE PROJECT

02-5-1 When to Close

There are three main types of project closure — all should follow a formal procedure, but the emphasis of the procedure will depend on what type of closure is occurring:

- Project termination (ahead of anticipated schedule)
- Project completion
- Project handover (where management and responsibility are transferred).

The decision as to whether a project is ready for closure is usually taken by the client or sponsor, and is not always self-evident. For instance with a termination, the client may have to weigh:

- Political factors (the loss of face consequent upon early termination)
- Economic considerations (perhaps an extra financial burden has been placed upon the project by changes in the macro-environment, or at the micro level, there may be prohibitive costs associated with salvaging a project which has gone awry);
- Human resource factors (if the project ends prematurely, the project team will be difficult to re-deploy)
- Technical issues (projects which are reliant on technology may find themselves overtaken by rival developments).

CASE STUDY

In 1990 a small publishing company took the decision to develop a board game to tie in with a series of academic publications for secondary schools. The response to the pilot version of the game was excellent — the best feedback the company had received for any trial product — and this prompted the directors to agree an unprecedented investment in producing and marketing the board game.

Early sales were brisk, but then a change to the national curriculum invalidated the series of publications associated with the board game. Although the game had been devised to stand apart from this series, the company's marketing campaign had firmly established the link. The result was that the company had hundreds of remaindered book titles, and thousands of unsold board games. The latter was a far more galling prospect given the size of the investment in producing the board game, and the significant cost of storing its components.

ACTION **ACTIVITY 10**

Summarize the options facing the publishing company.

02-5

Compare your response with our commentary in Appendix 1.

In fact the company opted to hang on to the stock and tried twice without success to re-launch the product. One of the key influencing factors upon that decision was the value of the stock which was a significant asset on the company's balance sheet.

Project termination then, can be an agonizing process. Project completion will be a more straightforward prospect provided a project has clearly defined objectives, stages and deliverables. However, although a completed project has successfully negotiated all stages and gates between initiation and closure, it does not follow that the project itself has been wholly successful. One only has to think of some of the major UK projects — Concorde, Canary Wharf, Eurotunnel – to appreciate that even projects which go way over budget and schedule can be compelled to complete when most others would be terminated. With high profile projects like these, the impetus tends to be political.

Project handover can be as difficult to manage as termination:

☞ Research and development projects will often tread water or dissolve into inertia, even though they have reached a perfectly viable end point. The difficulty is usually associated with getting someone to implement the research findings or go into production with the prototype.

☞ Many construction projects founder when the built facility needs to be sold or occupied. The London dockland developments of the late 1980s are a good example of a project which failed to execute a successful transfer between builder and owner.

☞ Unscrupulous project managers may deliberately fudge the issue of handover in order to guarantee income over a longer term. For instance, a specialist web developer may be commissioned to develop a site which can be maintained by internal staff once it is up and running. But unless the developer is scrupulous about building in simple templates and arranging comprehensive training for internal staff, the commissioning organization may find itself paying for specialist support well after the website has been launched.

In summary, project clients and managers need to have a clear vision right from the initial project definition, of what the project's end point will be. They also need to have clearly defined deliverables and responsibilities for each key project stage so that objective evaluation and transfer can be carried out efficiently. Clarity in these definitions is the best safeguard against the dissolving or never-ending project.

www.universal-manager.co.uk

02-5-2   A Procedure for Project Closure

Once the decision has been taken to close a project, the closure procedure should take effect. In ideal circumstances, the closure will be of the 'completion' type and a standard closure procedure will have been circulated among key players (particularly project team members) at the end of the 'specify' or planning stage of the project.

However, most projects do not enjoy ideal circumstances and it is far more likely that one or more of the following statements will be true:

☞   No closure procedure has been devised or circulated
☞   The project has had to be terminated abruptly
☞   Closure has been agreed between the client and project manager, but few others are privy to this decision
☞   The full implications of project closure have not been considered in detail.

The first thing that therefore needs to happen once a closure decision has been reached is to inform anyone involved in the project who:

☞   Is dependent upon project continuation or upon specified outputs
☞   May authorize project expenditure
☞   Might otherwise continue working on the project.

Formal and detailed notification of project closure is not necessary — the information given should be sufficient to explain that work and expenditure on the project has ceased. Preparing comprehensive documentation about project closure is the next stage of the procedure: reporting closure.

02-5

 **ACTIVITY 11**

Note down the key sections you would include in a closure report for a project which you have been managing.

Now read on.

Closure Report

Typically, project closure will be reported under the following headings.

(1)   Project title

(2)   Key players at project closure
      Detailing the roles played

(3)   Project objectives

(4)   Closure statement
      This should make clear why the project is being closed, and who has authorized closure. For terminated projects, this is the place to indicate whether there is any likelihood of the project being re-started. For handover projects, an overview of the transfer should be provided, stating who is relinquishing control, who is taking it over and how the transfer relates to the overall project plan.

(5)   Project achievements
      An outline statement of the main project achievements related to agreed:
      ☞ *Objectives*
      ☞ *Budget*
      ☞ *Schedule*
      ☞ *Quality specification*
      ☞ *Other standards.*

(6)   Outstanding issues
      Stating:
      ☞ *Key objectives and standards the project has failed to fulfil*
      ☞ *Any of the above which still need to be met: how this will happen, who will be accountable (they should have agreed to this), and the timescale in which these matters will be resolved*
      ☞ *Proposals for redeploying or scrapping remaining resources.*

(7)   Project efficiency
      This will be a more detailed statement (probably supported by appendices) of:
      ☞ *Actual costs against budget (down to the level of key project stages)*
      ☞ *Actual resource consumption against the project plan (also to stage level)*
      ☞ *Actual progress against schedule (also to stage level).*

(8)   Project outputs
      Here the report should itemize all products and by-products of the project (again, appendices may be necessary). Products will include documentation such as designs and drawings, and may also extend to intangibles such as new partnerships, new markets or intellectual property.

Lock (1998) provides much guidance relevant to this section of the closure report in the final chapter of 'Project Management'. He is particularly concerned with the 'as-built conditions' of construction, engineering and manufacturing projects — it is noteworthy that not only are final designs and specification documents required to be itemized, but also all revisions and modifications.

(9)   Lessons learned.
We will return to this key heading shortly.

The report may be delivered at a formal closure meeting at which the client, project manager, key stakeholders and project team members should be present. The chief purpose of the meeting will be to present the closure report and gain agreement to its content from all parties.

From a political perspective, the report and closure meetings are crucial and the astute project manager will wish to control both so that success is celebrated and failure played down or attributed elsewhere. A more altruistic approach will treat the report and, especially the meeting, as opportunities to obtain 360 degree feedback on project performance in order to identify lessons which may benefit future projects (there is a case for holding the meeting before the report is compiled).

02-5

However, like it or not, political considerations are usually to the fore at the end of most projects — especially in project or programme-oriented organizations. As they have had throughout the life of the project, the key players will have divergent interests at project closure:

☛   The project manager may want to be assigned now to a bigger, higher profile project. He will certainly want the project to be viewed as a success.
☛   The client's primary interest may be in establishing accurate data on project efficiency and outputs, in acquiring all outputs (including by-products), or perhaps in ensuring that the loose ends are tied up.
☛   Senior management stakeholders will be keen to gain repeat or continued business from the client, and might also have serious concerns about how surplus resources are to be disposed of.
☛   Project team members may share the project manager's desire to receive credit and avoid blame, and they will also be concerned about re-deployment.

In terminated or handover projects, political manoeuvring is almost inescapable at this juncture: with the former type, there may be an unseemly stampede to avoid being associated with failure, while the latter type may bring current and imminent project managers into direct conflict over timing, resourcing and accountability details.

02-5-3   Lessons Learned

Many enlightened organizations today practise knowledge management. Two of the key tenets of this emerging discipline are:

(1)   The knowledge an organization gains through its work must be valued as an asset which will contribute to future business success.
(2)   The knowledge asset should be made available to others within the organization.

In a nutshell, this is also the rationale behind ensuring that lessons are learned from projects — whether successes or failures.

It should be reasonably clear what we may learn from a project: examination of the management and operational processes, tools and methods employed throughout the project will be enlightening; structure and infra-structure will be worthy of close study; appraisal of sub-contractor and team performance should inform future contracting arrangements; the way critical relationships were managed is likely to hold useful lessons; the list could go on for quite a while.

Less evident though is how to make sure that genuinely useful lessons are really learned by the people who should take most heed. There can often be a curious reluctance to revisit the recent past of a just closed project. We may attribute this to a number of different factors:

☛   Key people are genuinely too busy to pause and reflect
☛   There may be a latent fear that the past holds unpalatable truths
☛   Where project lessons challenge ingrained assumptions or practices, it appears far easier to ignore them than to make radical changes
☛   With large projects which take place over long time periods, during which key personnel leave and are replaced, it can be difficult for those overseeing closure to obtain an accurate picture of how the total project was conducted
☛   Often, the problem lies with the way the lessons are presented — an abrasive, finger-pointing style will immediately warn people off, while an over elaborate style with too much detail will ensure that no-one reads the document.

Faced with such steep barriers to learning, it will be difficult to ensure that important lessons from a project do permeate. Organizations that are culturally pre-disposed to learning and knowledge management will have standard processes and systems in place to capture such lessons:

☞ Frequent project reviews convened soon after the events to which they relate, and involving all those who contributed to those events (often such sessions are informal)
☞ Networked databases into which 'fresh knowledge' will be input, for retrieval by anyone in the organization with the requisite authority
☞ 360 degree feedback where the project manager will invite the views of client, stakeholders, team members and possibly end users and sub-contractors
☞ Standard reporting formats to capture project lessons (the simpler the better!)

Organizations that do not attempt to introduce similar approaches, and where a 'blame culture' is allowed to fester, will be doomed to repeat mistakes, until a really serious one occurs — by then it may be too late!

02-5

APPENDIX 1

COMMENTARY ON ACTIVITIES

Activity 5

There are three main arguments against concurrency:

(a)   It constrains the design or specification stage by requiring that each component be designed individually. The implication is that designers are unable to experiment for fear of producing designs that are incompatible with components already built.

(b)   It prohibits refinement of the whole design (which might achieve greater efficiency or effectiveness for the product as a whole).

(c)   It means that designers and builders are working separately, with only formalized reference to each other — this lack of interchange is likely to result in unimaginative outcomes delivered at a pedestrian pace.

Activity 7

A skeleton scoping brief for the Channel Tunnel project might have looked something like this.

Purpose	Key Players	
Link UK and Continental Europe by road and rail	*Client:*	UK and French governments
	Sponsor:	Various banks and major investors
	Stakeholders:	Small investors, rail and ferry operators, local government in Kent and Nord Pas de Calais
	Project team:	Eurotunnel, Transmanche-Link, various sub-contractors
End results	**Standards**	
☛ Increase in trade between UK and Continental Europe ☛ Increase in travel between UK and European destinations ☛ Decline in ferry operator sector ☛ Improved road and rail infrastructure in vicinity of tunnel	☛ Safety (for construction workers, shuttle operators and passengers) ☛ Profitability (for Channel Tunnel Group and its investors) ☛ Quality (of tunnel construction, road and rail links, etc.) ☛ Politics — the project must be visibly successful in meeting its deadline and attracting investors	

Activity 9

You may have suggested some of the following consequences:

- ☛ Failure to foresee critical interventions
- ☛ Failure to secure necessary resources
- ☛ Poor or inappropriate communication with key players
- ☛ Project success may go unrecognized
- ☛ Project setbacks may be capitalized upon by more astute rivals
- ☛ Lack of support for the project from influential figures
- ☛ Failure to detect and deal with unproductive conflict between key players
- ☛ Limited influence and control for the project manager.

Activity 10

In terms of our basic project life cycle, the board game project moved into the 'implement' stage once the decision was made to invest in production and marketing. If the early success had been maintained, the cycle of production, sales and marketing might have continued merrily, keeping the project alive and still in implementation.

However, the national curriculum change forces the issue, and the directors are faced with two clear alternatives:

- ☛ Re-launch the board game, either disassociated from the original publication series or connected to a new series
- ☛ Close the project and write off the stock.

www.universal-manager.co.uk

APPENDIX 2

GLOSSARY

Change Control
Registering all potential modifications to the project: analysing their potential impact; and comprehensively identifying the consequences of any change. Also known as Variation Control.

Close Out
Completion of work once the project has been implemented.

Communication
Effective transmission and receipt of information in all available formats and media.

Configuration Management
An extension of Change Control, focussing on control of the technical configuration of a project.

Conflict Management
The art of managing conflict creatively.

Control and Co-ordination
Establishing targets, measuring actual performance, establishing variance and instituting necessary corrective action. Ensuring coherence and 'fit' between the work of various project participants, in line with overall project objectives.

Cost Control
The discipline of reconciling planned and actual money or time figures to physical parts of the project.

Delegation
The practice of getting others to perform work effectively which one chooses not to do oneself.

Estimating
Making a quantified assessment of the resources required to implement part or all of a project.

Finance
In a project context, finance is essentially the process of raising and managing the allocation of funds.

Industrial Relations
Management of the work-force, including, but not limited to, statutory responsibilities and duties, negotiating terms and conditions of pay and employment, union and non-union relations, and manpower planning.

Information Communication Technology (ICT)
Collective term for all automated systems used to transmit data: includes mobile telephones, the Internet, e-mail, video conferencing, digital television, etc.

Information Technology (IT)
Usually computer based technology for the collection, storage, processing and presentation of data.

Integration
Co-ordinating and controlling people, resources, processes and functions which may be dispersed geographically, functionally, temporally or hierarchically.

Law
The legal duties, rights and processes which govern a project situation. There are several different categories of law. The most important include national legal systems, such as criminal law, but particularly company and commercial law, employment laws, contract law, health and safety and other regulatory requirements such as planning law, data protection, sexual and racial discrimination building regulations, etc.

Leadership
Organizing, planning, controlling and directing resources. Motivating the project team.

Management Accounting
Allocating costs correctly to provide a clear view of current and forecast financial performance.

Marketing and Sales
Matching the capacity of an organization with the needs/desires of its client base to bring about the maximum possible advantage for both parties, then getting someone to buy the product or service being offered by the company.

Management Development
Staff planning, recruitment, development, training and assessment.

Mobilization
The initiation of project work typically involves bringing together project personnel and securing equipment and facilities. The term 'Project Start-Up' is often used to cover the same period.

Negotiation
Attempting to achieve your own desired outcome from a transaction, while leaving all other parties equally satisfied at the subsequent outcome.

Operations and Technical Management
Management of the physical resources (usually labour, equipment and materials) required for design and production of a product or service.

Organization Design
Design of the most appropriate organizational structure for a project.

Performance Measurement
Measurement of a project's progress in relation to planned cost and schedule, sometimes using the calculation of Earned Value.

Planning
Creation of a project plan which details the project purpose, objectives, strategy, standards, key players, task breakdown, resource allocation, schedule and milestones.

Portfolio
A group of projects managed by the same organization, team or individual, which are not necessarily aligned towards the same strategic objective.

Post Project Appraisal
Usually carried out once a project's outputs or end results are in use. Chief purpose is to provide feedback in order to identify key lessons learned which can benefit future projects.

Procurement
Can include: an investment appraisal into the options available; procurement or acquisition strategy; preparation of contract documentation; acquisition; selection of suppliers; administration of contracts; and storage, inspection, expediting and handling of materials and equipment.

Programme
A group of projects which together contribute to the achievement of the same strategic objective.

Programme Management
Management of a suite of strategically aligned projects.

Project
A non-routine piece of work undertaken to deliver:
- ☛ A beneficial result
- ☛ Of a specified quality
- ☛ Within defined time and cost constraints
- ☛ And which contains an element of risk.

Project Appraisal
Calculating the viability of the project — will include financial, environmental, health & safety and performance appraisals.

Project Environment
All external influences which may be brought to bear on a project.

Project Life Cycle
The sequence of phases through which a project will pass from conception to completion.

Project Management
Planning, organization, monitoring and control of all aspects of a project, plus the motivation of all involved to achieve the project objectives safely and within agreed time, cost and performance criteria.

Project Strategy
High level, comprehensive definition of how a project will be developed and managed.

Project Success/Failure Criteria
The UK Association for Project Management (APM) identifies three different types of criteria:
☛   Those of the project sponsor or client
☛   Time, budget, and specification
☛   Profitability.

Quality
Assuring that required standards of performance are attained. Includes: defining a Quality policy; establishing a system for Quality management; Quality Assurance (QA) which defines procedural and documentation requirements; Quality Control (QC) — the process of measuring whether a pre-defined level of performance has indeed been achieved.

Risk Analysis and Measurement
Risk Management is the process of identification, assessment, analysis and management of all project risks.

Safety
Determining standards and methods to minimize the likelihood of accident or damage to people and equipment. Ensuring that these standards are respected in operation, and reviewing them to ensure their continued validity.

Scheduling
Selecting and applying the most appropriate techniques to create a timetable for delivery of project outputs on time and to specification.

Sub-project
A work package for which responsibility has been delegated to someone other than the leader of the overall project.

Systems and Procedures
These detail the standard methods, practices and processes for handling frequently occurring events within the project.

Systems Management
Prime activities are Systems Analysis, Systems Design and Engineering and Systems Development.

Team Building
Assembling the right project team, and creating a co-operative environment.

Value Analysis
Application of a series of analytical techniques to an existing product, process or organization.

Value Engineering
Application of a series of proven techniques during the concept and design stages of a project.

Value Management
A structured means of improving business effectiveness in line with strategic goals: may incorporate techniques such as Value Engineering and Value Analysis.

Variation Control
See 'Change Control'.

Work Definition
The definition of project work and organization is achieved through the use of a Work Breakdown Structure (WBS) and an Organization Breakdown Structure (OBS).

Work Package
A component of the project: a piece of work contributing to project objectives, and which may be coupled with other work packages.

APPENDIX 3

USEFUL RESOURCES

W H Aitken (1997/98), *Project Management & Operations Research*, South Bank University London.

Project Magazine, produced by the Association for Project Management.

N M L Barnes (1990), *Financial Control*, Thomas Telford Publications.

R Buttrick (1997), *The Project Workout*, Pitman Publishing.

J Chalmers (1997), *Managing Projects*, How To Books.

C Chapman & S Ward (1998), *Project Risk Management*, Wiley.

R K Corrie (1990), *Project Evaluation*, Thomas Telford Publications.

M A Cusumano & K Nobeoka (1998), *Thinking Beyond Lean*, The Free Press.

S Ghoshal & C A Bartlett (1998), *The Individualized Corporation*, William Heinemann.

P O Gaddis (1959), 'The Project Manager', *Harvard Business Review*.

G Johnson & K Scholes (1988), *Exploring Corporate Strategy*, Prentice Hall.

R L Kliem & I S Ludin (1992), *The People Side of Project Management*, Gower.

B P Lientz & K P Rea (1998), *Project Management for the 21st Century*, Academic Press.

D Lock (1998), *Project Management*, Gower.

H Mintzberg (1979), *The Structuring of Organizations*, Prentice Hall.

P W G Morris (1997), *The Management of Projects*, Thomas Telford Publications.

T Peters & R Waterman (1982), *In Search of Excellence*, Harper & Row.

G Reiss (1996), *Programme Management Demystified*, E & F N Spon.

P M Senge (1990), *The Fifth Discipline*, Century Business.

J R Turner (1993), *The Handbook of Project-based Management*, McGraw-Hill.

J Whatmore (1999), *Releasing Creativity*, Kogan Page.

J R Womack & D Ross (1990), *The Machine That Changed The World*, Maxwell Macmillan International.

WEBSITES

Association for Project Management
www.apm.org.uk
Project Management Resources
pmblvd.com
www.ccta.gov.uk/prince
www.pug.mcmail.com/pip/about-prince.html

APPENDIX 4

NEBS Management Diploma

NEBS Management is the Awarding Body for specialist management qualifications — committed to developing qualifications which meet the needs of today's managers at all levels across industry.

The NEBS Management Diploma is a broad management development programme aimed at practising and aspiring middle managers. It offers a comprehensive, integrated programme of personal and organizational development.

Content

During the Diploma programme, a candidate will:

☞ Establish a Personal Development Plan
☞ Study theory and practice in the following key management areas:
  ☞ Managing Human Resources
  ☞ Financial Management
  ☞ Organizational Activities and Change
  ☞ Management Skills
☞ Produce a specialist Management Report
☞ Compile an Individual Development Portfolio.

Flexibility

The NEBS Management Diploma requires a minimum of 240 hours of study but can be completed on a full-time or part-time basis as appropriate. Many programmes will offer a mix of direct training, open learning and practical work-based activity. In connection with the Universal Manager series, the Diploma therefore offers the facility for learning in a variety of media including paper-based material, on-line resources and taught elements.

Assessment

Assessment of performance takes a rounded view of the capability demonstrated by the candidate in assignments and specialist tasks, in the management report and portfolio, and in interview.

Enrolment

The usual entry requirements are:

☞ At least two years' relevant management experience
☞ PLUS a NEBS Management Certificate, a Management S/NVQ at Level 3 or the equivalent qualification.

There are many Accredited Centres approved to offer the Diploma programme in the UK and abroad. Call NEBS Management on **0171 294 3053** for details of your nearest Centre.

INDEX

95